Birthmarks

Birthmarks

Poems

WHITNEY RIO-ROSS

RESOURCE *Publications* · Eugene, Oregon

BIRTHMARKS
Poems

Resource Publications
An Imprint of Wipf and Stock Publishers
199 W. 8th Ave., Suite 3
Eugene, OR 97401

www.wipfandstock.com

PAPERBACK ISBN: 978-1-7252-6172-3
HARDCOVER ISBN: 978-1-7252-6173-0
EBOOK ISBN: 978-1-7252-6174-7

Manufactured in the U.S.A.   02/19/20

for my mother

Unto the woman he said,
I will greatly multiply thy sorrow and thy conception;
in sorrow thou shalt bring forth children; and thy desire
shall be to thy husband, and he shall rule over thee.
    —Genesis 3:16

And the angel came in unto her, and said,
Hail, thou that art highly favoured, the Lord is with thee:
blessed art thou among women . . . Fear not, Mary:
for thou hast found favour with God. And, behold,
thou shalt conceive in thy womb, and bring forth a son . . .
The Holy Ghost shall come upon thee, and the power of
the Highest shall overshadow thee: therefore also that holy thing
which shall be born of thee shall be called the Son of God.
    —Luke 1:28, 30–31, 35

Contents

Acknowledgments

Many thanks to the journals in which these poems first appeared, sometimes in earlier versions or under other titles:

Adanna: "Eve, lover" (under the title "Eve")

America Magazine: "Mary, Pietà"

Reflections Journal: "Esther, playing house"

Rock & Sling: "Rachel, at Leah's baby shower" (under the title "At My Sister's Baby Shower")

So to Speak: "Eve, healer"

Waccamaw Journal: "Eve, creator"

All Bible quotations are taken from the King James Version. "Proverbs 31, as curse" is an erasure of Proverbs 31:10–30. "Magnificat, as plea" is an erasure of Luke 1:46–55. "Resurrection, as resurrection" is an erasure of John 20: 13–17. Erasure poems contain a few changes in punctuation and capitalization.

"Esther, playing house" is for Amanda Bennett.

"Elizabeth, invitation to John" is for November Lyn Howerton.

"Mary, Pietà" was inspired by a drawing by Chris E. W. Green.

Special thanks to poet Jason Adam Sheets, whose encouragement and guidance greatly helped this collection become what it is. Additional thanks to AWP's Writer to Writer Mentorship program for giving me the opportunity to learn from him.

My deepest gratitude to Joshua, my dear one, whose endless support and love make poetry possible.

I

PROVERBS 31, AS CURSE

Who can find a   woman? Her
            heart   shall have no need.

                                        All the days of her life
she seeketh   her hands
                like   food.

She   giveth   a portion

                                                    of her
                        loins
                                                    by night:
she layeth,
                                she reacheth,   needy.

She is   afraid of her household—

her husband,   the gates.

She openeth her mouth,   and   her tongue
                                                            eateth
                            up   her
            daughters.

A woman that feareth   shall be praised.

EVE, CREATOR

Half a day's pushing couldn't shove me into the world, so they snipped me from her stalk. The doctor tossed the hot potato to my father, who couldn't find the penis he'd promised himself. He delivered me to my mother's breasts, where I wouldn't taste her offering. I.V.'s take best to babies' heads, still soft enough for molding. But glass boxes can't hold cuddles, only holes drilled for her fingers to brush mine. We can't leave our grief rootless—we have to point our blame. When I stretched my toes, they pointed at her. Her first had spread back into the womb, dark and formless void, deaf to her questions at the ultrasound tech. What had she done   wrong   this   time? It was the first attempt to save my life, successful enough. But we bear our birthmarks—a sidestep from perfection, her constant reminder to give praise for what will mourn. The doctor told her it was a 50/50 chance I'd live through the week, lower still that I would grow into the girl who patted her next beach ball. "I remember being there. You fed me apple juice," I whispered, feeling for kicks. "She's full of apple juice."

HAGAR, WITH HER SON'S TEACHERS

He is wild.

He does not play
with the other children.

(They mean, *He does not look*
like the other children.)

He scratches the ground
outside the window, drags his name
through dust too dry to sustain
what he means. Does he remember
how it scorched his growing feet,
flightless for all their wheeling?

Is his father an angry man?
Is he
          still in the picture?

We are expected to answer
for our children, but strangers
cannot keep confessions:

(I took every scrap
that man gave me and wouldn't,
fled the only home my child had known.
Did you have better directions?)

No.

She can only whisper that she will
fix it, then do nothing that night
but let him sleep, chest swell
to collapse, breath heated like the
angel's mirage she saw as they crossed,
a vision she would have sworn by.

Tomorrow she should saddle
his neck with a plaque,
barely etched with a name
they fail to pronounce.

They must bow to read
the glaring brass mirror:

Look at me. Look at me. *Look.*

RACHEL, AT LEAH'S BABY SHOWER

You're next!
—I don't think I'll have—
You may change your mind.

Their laughs prophesy
a transformation of heart:
sacrifice youth for stretch marks,
measure of womanhood. *You can't*
resist what you are made for.

     She knows this is a lie.
     She wishes it were her lie.

The truth is each new moon's bloody
void devours her.
She cannot give her love
the lie he prays for: *You are*
enough. What we have is enough.

The truth is she's tired of grieving
ambiguous losses—ghosts
unheld, though not unnamed.
They have given them names.

The truth is she cannot hear
the story they would offer,
Sunday's scalding comfort
for the barren: the Lord promised
and purged a woman's doubt by miracle.

God does not lie. We must
always trust God's word.
She would hold her tongue as she does
now; it isn't tied by unbelief.

     The truth is
     she doesn't know that word.
     God made her no promises.

EVE, LOVER

For weeks, my eyes have blinked open to my mother's nightgown dangling from the hook of my skylight. I often hang laundry there, and though it only took an hour for the sheer chiffon to dry, I can't take it down. Every time I reach for it, my fingertips lose themselves in slow circles, rubbing the delicate cream fabric between them, caressing the long folds the way I imagine my father might have, but probably didn't. I took it from her when I visited over Christmas, having discovered it while cleaning her closet. Tucked between pants she might be able to wear again and sweaters I pray she won't, there it was: a garment made for Venus, elegant and seductive and nothing like my mother. I told her I was keeping it. She protested. I asked how many times she had worn it. Twice, maybe. I told her I would get more use out of it, and she blushed. But it just stays there,   floating above the foot of my bed. Meanwhile I spend the mornings watching the dawn glow through, translucent—

warming a body

I can't quite

recognize.

BATHSHEBA, LAUNDRY DAY

Three floods could not
dissolve him. Still that stench,
the beastly sour—his? hers?

How much had she absorbed
when he devolved her into darkness,
gaping nameless and unclaimed?

A cavity brimmed, she overflowed
and dripped his seed
with every waddle home.

Her mother taught her to wash
intimates by hand, save lace from hooks,
keep a cup's shape so it covers enough.

—what she hadn't warned her:
    some things can only be scratched out—

Now she gnarls her wrists,
wrings sweat from torn satin,
raws her palms clean of him.

And she'd give every fingernail
to claw out his stain and those eyes
that saw anything could be his.

ESTHER, PLAYING HOUSE

She learns what to want
before she finishes the alphabet—
B, boy. She needs to L love one of those.
Mother is M. Like M, she'll be a wife.
She doesn't know that letter,
but it must mean being wrapped
in white like the B bed sheet
she can't wear on Halloween.
No, a girl (that's G) means being wrapped
in glitter. Glitter turns G into a P princess.
Boys dress however they like,
but one told her they all carry swords
(S, same as snake). He kicked
playground pebbles at her shins
and yelled, "So we can get you!"
(How can U be P princess?)
At night, she places her favorite doll—
B again, beautiful—inside cardboard
walls, forehead balanced against
sliding glass doors. (No one
can always stand on tip-toe T.)
She's ready for nightmares—N, like nothing.
She sings her letters, spells a world of wishes
(she should learn that letter).
She'll keep up her P practice,
become P perfect.

EVE, HEALER

In my memory, she is holding her scrawl, stored on the yellow
legal pads bearing her patients' babbled fears. She clutches
mine, the one she carried to my appointments, hand racing to
catch everything the doctor said. One idea splintered to a
hundred questions, suggestions, tests—

maybe   *it could be,*
         we might try,   *keep an eye on her.*

She didn't believe in erasers or blank space; she covered every
page she could. At home, she asked me if I still saw the
tornados coming to swallow us, and when did my hands start
looking like that? Like all women, she hid her fears from what she
loved. Of course you washed cereal down with pink
potions of pretend cherries. Every brain had its terrors, and
surgeries helped us grow beyond them. Brilliant architect,
she scheduled check-ups between swim lessons and sleepovers,
fashioned my world plain enough that I never thought to
question it. Miraculous, how we imagine all lives look like
ours—until we discover others. When I woke to blood at
thirteen, I sprinted to her in soaked panties. Poised over
scribbles, she paused with a smile and promised all was as it
should be. When I slinked away, she crossed out a line,
hieroglyphed its margins, just to make sure she didn't leave
anything out.

DEBORAH, APPLICATION FOR PROMOTION

1. What do you like best about your current position?

> (*I like that my ears have learned*
> *to play a static every time*
> *a room applauds William for my idea.*)

I enjoy making decisions
with others for the overall
betterment of the community.

2. Why do you want to leave your current position?

> (*If I climb a few floors, Barry's hands*
> *couldn't reach my ass. If the elevator breaks,*
> *I'll take the stairs with my knees chained*
> *together—never give the devil a chance*
> *to eye me from a new angle.*)

I like to face new challenges.

3. Why do you want this new position?

> (*I want nothing new, only consolation*
> *for a marriage lost to late nights*
> *consumed by fluorescents. You can't*
> *direct-deposit Roy's squeeze on the shoulder.*)

The new position is the natural
progression from my current
responsibilities, which I have
dedicated the time to master.

4. Why should we consider you for this promotion?

> (*Consider it charity that I'm still here,*
> *the cosmos conspiring to ground me*
> *with custody battles and cheap childcare.*
> *Just look at what I've provided you.*)

> My previous work has prepared me
> to take on the extra leadership
> responsibilities. My portfolio contains
> the projects I have directed so far.

5. How would others in your department describe you?

> Helpful   (*You have a family to see—*
> *give the girl the rest.*
> *She won't complain.*)

> Loyal   (*She's a good girl, won't get*
> *you in trouble for a little fun.*)

> Strong   (*Bitch.*)

6. What obstacles or challenges have you overcome?

NAOMI, SKINNY DIPPING

She can't remember the last time
she undressed in such a dark rush.
It must have been before her skin rippled
with worries, before breasts drooped heavy
with all they'd given up.

It was probably a night like this,
fleeing a crowded house to do
what her parents wouldn't approve.
Only then, her laced fingers sweated
in tangled promises of young lovemaking.

Grief and age won't be left alone,
no matter if they need it most.
But night—night paints everyone
deserted, shelled in an unseen
they can't throw off.

She wants to tunnel through the pond
but shuffles to a still, no tow to pull her under.
Maybe she could choke on one of those
butter-drowned casseroles. God knows
there's enough for her own funeral.

If the preacher's still praying,
he could bless her soul over pecan pie—
no need for more ceremony at this hour.
Eventually, all cries yield to sleep,
unfinished as they may seem.

Bobbing the surface, her ears
flood with yesterdays—

> her holler at the boys' truck
> idled on the bank
> as radio thundered the kitchen

> their *Just one more! It's almost over!*

her husband's barrel out the door
to bluff a scolding and sing along

everyone's grins
and too-quick goodnight kisses

She can't remember the old tunes
they carried to bed, only the noise
left while they slept, all that's left now—
the cicadas' hummed hymns, somehow
still loud enough to raise the dead.

II

MAGNIFICAT, AS PLEA

And Mary said,

           Lord,

                  my Saviour,

        regard
   the   handmaiden.

                Call me blessed
                   and holy.

   Mercy,

   shew   strength with

               imagination—

   exalt   low degree,

   fill   the
             empty

        servant

              for ever.

MARY, ANNUNCIATION

Dripping gold, you began
a pink cross. My spine curved
a question over the bowl,
first morning's retch
to expel all doubt.

How could I expect you
in prophecies—
charts mapping life's chances,
death's law? Unbridled
anchor, you plunged ahead,
racing to a bed beyond my dive.

I had learned how to die
alone, no hand to release,
no name to forget. I had learned
to name *impossible* a blessing.

How
do you name
a dying blessing?

Still, my love, I must confess:
my heart's leap knowing yours
was there—

as if you might resurface.

ELIZABETH, INVITATION TO JOHN

We always measure you by fruit, sweet
and sticky one. For now, you are
a peach of possibilities, but this much we know:

Your plush folding into form, covered
in our animal fuzz, is destined for bruises
and blisters, your blinded eyes made to behold
our brutal world. You will learn hunger
and thirst, those cravings we have endured
so you would not want.

Curls and tangles today, your limbs
will stretch past their limits with nails
made for cleaving closer.
May you be held until you squirm
free to fling yourself wild in all the ways
our mothers warn us not to.

You will most certainly hiccup.
This much we know.

But here in war, riot, rot—we hope
the heavens for you, that should science
be right, you can hear the good in us,
can recognize this voice, already trust
those who have named you.

We hope you hear our *Welcome*.
May your cries be an anthem:
> *I am here.*
> *Let me bless this place.*

THE PRODIGAL'S MOTHER, WAITING

She loads the grocery cart
with contraband—chips, donuts,
everything he'd loved but couldn't have.
Their dinners have grown,
though they all eat less.

Her husband is a praying man,
freezing forks mid-journey
to pronounce a blessing before
turning beggar, his *thank you*
hovering over empty hands.

The man deserves some comfort—
call it *God* if he needs to.
But she won't ask for a miracle.
Please sounds too much like *if.*
There's no breathing in *if.*

If can't hold a bowl of cereal
sweet enough to turn him home.
If can't search the attic for comics
confiscated when he failed algebra.
There can be no *if,* only *when.*

When changes his sheets
every Tuesday. *When* sets four plates
on the table. *When* unlocks the door
while his father sleeps. *When* dozes
in the chair by the front window—

sure he isn't too far off, sure
he won't miss another morning.

MARY, DISPUTATION

Each blink was an enemy,
invitation for your absence
and my clawing dread.

    Had you been a normal child,
        would I have accepted losing you?

Your voice led my way,
always telling strangers
stories I hadn't taught you.

They grinned at my trembles,
but a glance at your bruised wrists
and bandaid collage revealed

their sin. Unashamed,
I slumped beside you,
shaping my fears as you waved

their embarrassed stumbles
goodbye with one hand,
squeezed mine with the other.

Before I could speak, you
explained, *You're a mom.*
You always find me.

    Had you been a normal child,
        I might have let you go.

WOMAN AT THE WELL, BETWEEN MEN

Whispers swarm her scarlet house,
whistling names she's trained
to answer, names lovers spit
over their shoulders as ash
pours down her throat,
their bodies returned to dust.

Whatever they call her,
the neighbors have one thing right—
she is waiting for the next one.
Addicted to it, they say.
It's hard to know.

She wishes she had stolen desire
from songs, film—but she has no scenes,
only the imprecise color of light
behind closed eyelids, a guess
at what might be beyond her.
Inarticulate as water sprinkling skin.

She's never had a word for it,
except
    maybe
    or *not this*
    or *never.*

For now, she'll brave the windows
framing today's failure,
tend the garden, hope
she finds the right translation
before another finds her.

MARTHA, AT THE HARVEST

Every year, her father grows too much corn,
drops bags at her feet with a *Get going*,
then returns to gather it shucked sooner
than a butterfly can catch its breath.
Her fingers have mastered the art of weaving,
a flutter so fast they forget how to stop.

Do you have anything else?
is a man's *I need more.*

She grieves her mother's kitchen,
brimming boiled water and yellow towers
he'll expect vanished before his hunger hits.
The woman's sure to burn her hands, let knuckles welt
in the name of finishing the damned thing,
make room for peace in this house.

A girl's exhaustion risks sin.
Hers is a glance heavenward, stopped short
at a robin's flourish and fall to nest and eggs.
Chest blushed against her glory,
she waits for the screech of gratitude,
announcing she has made something wonderful.

Weary hands abandon the moment, toss husks
to this queen as their silks confetti the air.
Maybe they will be accepted as gift,
a humble burst for creation before
she bends back to her gold and its worms,
wondering how you count enough.

MARY, PIETÀ

Body betrayed, I bore
the world's fugitive, had lost you
before we untethered.

Death is a matter of waiting,
and I saw yours curled
like a snake around every
corner, mine the spider
I couldn't catch in time.

When offered your marbled
flesh—
            I couldn't.

Forgive me. A mother can
only hold so many scars.

But hovered between nightmare
and waking, my wounds sink
into yours, fresh and warm
as I remember you. In darkness,
all blood sheds embraced.

This is how we began.

MARY MAGDALENE, AT DAYBREAK

The allure of sunrise always escaped her.
Perhaps those who abandon

dreams for better views, who must comfort
sleepless hours with purpose, delude themselves

with visions worth believing.
They insist the sky is not a color

swirled together by children's fingerpaints,
but the bright palette they hoped for.

Yet she too wanders dawn for this hush—
the dead's hilltop slumber.

Daybreak has its gifts, even if not from above.
People should look down more, he'd told her,

head shaking as her feet crushed petals
scattered at someone else's loss.

He was right.

The moment after the sun struggles up is
the moment to bow your head and witness

life warm to itself, color aching into the shadows.
This—this justifies the dark climb

into the earth's rafters, to behold its waking,
her secret she'll watch the world discover.

RESURRECTION, AS RESURRECTION

Woman, why weepest thou?
Because they have taken.

Woman, why weepest thou?

If thou have,
I will take.

I am
brethren.

Say   to my Father,   *Father.*
And to my God,   God.

EVE AND MARY, EMMAUS

She knows what she wants, but today she needs this charade of deliberation, weighing uncounted calories. Her eyes will land anywhere but mine. We can't face some questions. *Have you considered—*? Regret chokes her. *—I'm sorry.* For her, those words are not the stutter at nothing else to say, but a fist gripping syllables until confession bleeds out. The world can preach pardon and innocence for a mother's lifetime without her hearing it, even my *It's okay, Mom.* Her gaze floats to the next table, where I assume a child plays with their food. Shushed giggles and jingling plates reveal enough. I don't mean to turn away from children. It's like breathing—

Unconscious.
    Instinct.
        Survival.

But I can't avoid the arm thrust over our table, offering biscuit soaked in God knows what. Still the good grandma, she accepts, cheerily braced for the worst. At first nibble, he escapes with her laugh. Folding her lips together, she savors whatever mystery she holds, then yields my portion.

Let's just have more of this.

www.ingramcontent.com/pod-product-compliance
Lightning Source LLC
Chambersburg PA
CBHW071801020426
42331CB00008B/2358